The Spelling Skills Handbook

for the Word Wise

JOHN BARWICK

JENNY BARWICK

Pembroke Publishers Limited

Pembroke Publishers
538 Hood Road
Markham, Ontario, Canada L3R 3K9
www.pembrokepublishers.com

Distributed in the U.S. by Stenhouse Publishers
P.O. Box 360
York, Maine 03909
www.stenhouse.com

Canadian Cataloguing in Publication Data

Barwick, John, 1953-
    The spelling skills handbook for the word wise

Includes index.
ISBN 1-55138-118-4

1. English language — Orthography and spelling — Juvenile literature. I. Barwick, Jenny.
II. Title.

PE1145.2.B378 2000   428.1   C99-932861-1

Designed by Jane Schneider
Page composition by Adriana Alvarez and Angela Hempstead
Illustrated by Adriana Alvarez

Canadian Editors: Linda Hart-Hewins, Elaine Rubinoff, Robert Glen, Carol-Ann Freeman
Cover Desigh: John Zehethofer
Typesetting: Jay Tee Graphics Ltd.

Printed and Bound in Canada
9 8 7 6 5 4 3 2 1

Contents

Content

Part 4 Spelling to rule

Contents

Wotz the yoose of spelin?

To the student

The main 'yoose' of 'spelin' is to make it easy for people to understand what you write. Being able to spell well is a skill you will use for the rest of your life.

Why you write, how often you write and the 'audience' you write for, vary enormously. At school you write for your teacher and other students. Later, when you are working, you may need to write reports for your boss, fill in applications for jobs or write letters to other companies. At home you may need to leave messages for someone and write letters and messages on the Internet. In all these situations, good spelling is essential to get your message across.

Some people think that computers and spell checkers have made it less important to know how to spell. This is wrong. While these devices can be helpful, they are no substitute for spelling skills. You will still need good spelling skills and knowledge of words to choose the correct spelling from the ones the computer suggests. Spell

checkers do not pick up errors in usage, such as the wrong use of 'there' or 'their'.

This book gives you the tools to help you become a good speller. It will show you thirteen strategies you can use to learn how to spell words or to work out how words are spelled. You can also read about all the main spelling rules and the handy lists of commonly confused words and words grouped by theme or topic, will help you expand your own personal word bank.

To the teacher and parent

Learning to spell correctly is vital for any student who wants to produce good written English. This book is written in the belief that the teaching of spelling should be explicit and systematic. The skills taught in *Spelling Skills* enable students to approach spelling strategically. Thirteen effective spelling strategies, catering to different learning styles, are explained.

Spelling Skills sheds light on the common spelling rules, while offering background information about the history of the English language and how the roots of different words affect their letter structure and plural form.

Finally, a comprehensive set of lists is provided as a reference for students, enabling them to locate particular words they wish to spell or other words containing a particular letter combination.

Theme lists support classroom studies in Science, Environmental Science, Design and Technology, English, Visual Arts, Health and Physical Education.

Techniques to help students evaluate and monitor their own spelling progress

Timely and relevant evaluation techniques help students improve their spelling skills and transfer the spelling knowledge they have learned to their everyday writing activities. To be successful, students need to see the relevance of accurate spelling to their daily lives. They need to have lots of time to practise, see many accurate models, have regular feedback about their work and see that they are making progress. They need to learn to spell words that they feel are important to them.

To help students see the relevance of spelling, encourage them to develop their own personal spelling lists and dictionaries. It is the responsibility of students to compile a list of words from their everyday writing activities that they have difficulty remembering. Lists of words can also be part of a student's writing folder. In order not to overwhelm the students, the lists should be kept to ten or twelve words. It is the responsibility of students to check that these words are spelled correctly before any peer or teacher writing conference occurs. As a word is regularly spelled correctly, the word is crossed off the list and another word is added. Students can clearly see when they are making progress.

A range of rewards that allow students to advance to a more difficult level of words can be powerful motivation. In order to highlight progress, teachers should always be careful to mark the number of words correctly spelled versus the number not spelled correctly. It can be helpful to have students graph the number of words correctly spelled as a concrete way to help them see their progress. As students see their spelling improve, they will transfer this skill more readily to their everyday writing.

Why is spelling important?

The benefits of being a good speller

Being a good speller brings many benefits.

Good spellers approach their writing confidently because they know they can spell most of the words they want to use.

Good spellers write quickly because they don't have to hesitate often over the spelling of the words they write.

Dear Grandma,

We went to the coast on the weekend.

Dad told us about navigation at sea.

We ate fish and chips later and

mom had crustaceans, which are

shellfish like prawns and lobster.

I want to be a sailor when I grow up.

love, Lucy.

Good spellers don't have to stick to the small range of words that they are sure they can spell when they are writing. This results in writing that is more interesting to read and often more accurate in its meaning.

What makes a good speller?

🙂 Good spellers have strategies that help make spelling easier.

🙂 Good spellers break down a long word into small parts, which are easier to spell.

🙂 Good spellers develop their own 'tricks' to remember words they find hard but need to know how to spell.

🙂 Good spellers often know some of the spelling rules and how to use them.

🙂 Good spellers know how to check their spelling by using a dictionary.

🙂 Good spellers are not afraid to ask someone else how to spell a word.

🙂 Good spellers are confident writers because they know that the correct spelling of most words is something they already know, can work out or can find out.

AN ISLAND IS LAND

Is English a tricky language for spellers?

Words in the English language can be a bit tricky to spell, even for good spellers. In many languages each letter or letter group always represents the same sound. For example, in Italian the letters **'ce'** *always* make a **'che'** sound, like we use in the word **'chess'**. This means that once you know the sound for each letter or letter group, you can spell any word correctly just from the way it sounds — provided it is pronounced correctly, of course!

Unfortunately this is not the case in English. In English there may be many different ways of representing one sound.

Here is an example to show how different letters can represent the same sound. All the letter groups in the following words are pronounced the same way.

the **a** in **share**

the **ai** in **hair**

the **e** in **there**

the **ea** in **pear**

the **ei** in **heir**

Here is another example.

the **i** in **pin**

the **o** in **women**

the **y** in **hymn**

Other words, such as **pair** and **pear**, sound the same but have different meanings and different spellings. These words are called **homonyms**.

It is interesting to look at why English contains so many different sounds for the same letters and different spelling for words with the same sound. In fact understanding why this happens can help us become better spellers. Just read on ...

English — the 'vacuum cleaner' language

A vacuum cleaner?

Some people say that English is like a vacuum cleaner. Over the centuries it has picked up lots of bits and pieces (or words) from all over the world. Some words have been 'sucked into' English after invasions of Britain by other peoples. New words have also come into English through friendly contact with people who speak other languages.

English is a very old language. In fact no one knows just how old our language is. Tribes that lived in Britain many thousands of years ago spoke a very early form of our language, which we would not recognize as English now. Two thousand years ago invaders from Rome arrived, bringing with them their language, Latin. Latin, in turn, contained some words from Ancient Greek. English people began to use Latin words and their language changed greatly.

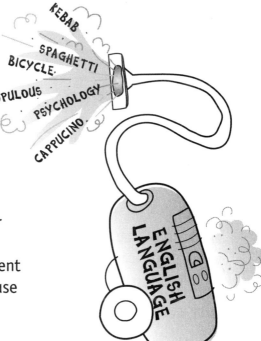

GERMANY SCANDINAVIA
700-1000AD

NORMANDY
1066AD

ROME
20BC

More changes occurred between 700 AD and 1000 AD as tribes from Germany and Scandinavia invaded most of Britain. Then in 1066 Normans from France invaded, which resulted in the addition of many French words to English. In fact, for many years, French was the language of the English ruling classes.

More recently, other words have come into English from other languages; words such as **spaghetti** (Italy), **smorgasbord** (Swedish), **bungalow** (the Hindi language, India) and **satay** (Malay). This is becoming more common as modern communication and more travel means people from different places exchange ideas and words more readily.

One of the reasons spelling in English can be difficult is that when new words are 'sucked' in they keep their foreign spelling and spelling patterns. Because of this there can be different ways of representing (or spelling) the same sounds.

JE SUIS LE KING

In North America, our branch of English is also influenced by First Nations languages. The names for many objects and implements have come from different Native languages. Some examples include **mukluk**, **igloo**, **muskeg**, **kayak** (all from the Inuit), **totem** (Chippewa and Algonquin) and **toboggan** (Micmac).

Other words have been brought by people who have come to live here. **Pizza** and **cappucino** are Italian while **kebab** comes from Arabic.

English is changing

IN SOOTH, I KNOW NOT WHY I AM SO SAD...

The English language we speak today is very different from the English of thousands of years ago, or even 150 years ago. If we were to go back in time 1000 years and listen to English people speaking English, we would probably think we were hearing a foreign language! This is because our language is constantly changing and developing.

Why do languages change?

The way people live and their knowledge and understanding of the world changes over time. This is one of the main reasons that languages change. New words are needed to describe new inventions or ideas, new ways of living and new ways of working.

For example, very new words such as **modem** and **Internet** were created to describe recent inventions that have now become a part of modern life. Earlier this century words such as **radio**, **automobile** and **airplane** were made up to describe new technology.

Some new words are mainly used by small groups of people. Scientists, for example, use many words in the course of their work that the rest of us may not understand. For example, the scientific name for a dog is **canis familiaris**. However, other recently coined scientific words, such as **ecosystem**, have become a part of everyday language because they describe things or phenomena with which many people are familiar.

In the same way that new words are needed for new inventions and ideas, many older words are no longer needed as the ideas or technology they refer to disappear from everyday life or become outdated. The use of these words has gradually died out. Some examples of words that are falling into disuse are:

Word	Meaning
florin	an old coin, worth two shillings (20 cents)
pint	a measure of liquid volume (about 600 mL)
radiogram	an old-fashioned combined radio and record player in a large cabinet
telegram	an early type of fax

Words can also change in meaning over time.

700 YEARS AGO - NICE

Seven hundred years ago the word **nice** meant foolish or stupid.

500 YEARS AGO - CEILING

600 YEARS AGO - SEWER

Six hundred years ago a **sewer** was a servant who arranged and tasted meals.

Five hundred years ago the word **ceiling** meant the lining of a wall, and then it came to mean a curtain or tapestry. Two hundred years later it was used to mean wooden planks lining the inside of a ship's hull, and eventually received its current meaning of the inside lining of a roof.

In the past the word **pencil** meant 'a paint brush' and 'a number of lines meeting at a point'.

The word **terrific** comes from the word 'terror', and really means 'causing great fear', but common usage and fashion has added another meaning. Now we often use it in everyday (colloquial) language to mean 'very good'.

The history of words

The history of words is called etymology. Knowing the history of a word can help to explain its spelling. Words that come from the same base language (root) often follow the same spelling rules and contain similar letter patterns.

Many of our words come from Greek, Latin (mainly through French words, but also some words surviving from the time when the

Romans invaded Britain), Old English (over 1000 years old), Old German (brought to Britain by invading tribes over a 1000 years ago), and French (which swamped the English language when it was brought in by the Normans in 1066).

The history of most words has been traced back to their roots. You can find brief word histories (etymologies) in good dictionaries and in special books called Dictionaries of Etymology, which give more detailed histories of words. Here are some examples of etymologies.

The word **book** comes from the Old English word **boc**. Its spelling has changed over time.

The word **cricket** came into English 600 years ago, from the French word **criquet**, meaning 'stick'.

The word **denim** comes from the French phrase **serge de Nimes**, meaning 'a strong cotton.' Denim was first made in Nimes, a city in France.

The word **telephone** comes from two ancient Greek words; **tele** meaning 'far off' and **phone** meaning 'sound or voice'.

The word **pumpkin** comes from the Greek word, **pepon** meaning 'a large melon.'

Greek and Latin word roots in English

Many English words can be traced back to two ancient languages, Latin and Ancient Greek. Both these languages, which are called the Classical languages, are now 'dead', as no one uses either in everyday speech or writing.

Ancient Greek has been replaced by Modern Greek and people from Rome (where Latin originated) now speak Italian. Both Modern Greek and Italian contain many words that can be traced back to the ancient languages.

Ancient Greek roots

The Ancient Greek civilization reached its peak about 2500 years ago. As well as a large number of everyday words that can be traced back to Ancient Greek, there are many
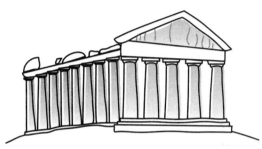
scientific and technical terms that have been coined from Ancient Greek roots.

The following examples all use Greek roots. The words marked with an asterisk (*) have been coined in the last 200 years from Greek roots:

⭐ words containing **ph** [making a /f/ sound] such as em**ph**asis, **ph**ysical, **ph**otograph* and tele**ph**one;*

⭐ words containing **ch** [making a /k/ sound] such as **ch**emical, stoma**ch**, s**ch**eme and te**ch**nical;

⭐ words containing **y** as a vowel, such as s**y**stem, Ol**y**mpic, st**y**le and t**y**pe;

⭐ words containing **eu** such as n**eu**rotic, pn**eu**monia and n**eu**tron;

⭐ words containing **au**, such as n**au**tical, thes**au**ras and tyrannos**au**rus;*

⭐ words beginning with a silent **p**, such as **p**neumonia, **p**sychic, **p**salm and **p**terodactyl.*

Latin roots

After the Greek civilization became less powerful, the Romans began to invade large parts of Europe, western Asia and North Africa. This became known as the Roman Empire. The Roman Empire was most powerful about 2000 years ago.

The language of the Romans, called Latin, was used by many people in the invaded lands. After the Romans left, Latin words remained in the local languages. The Romans occupied Britain from 43 AD until 410 AD.

The English language took in more Latin words in 1066, when people from Normandy in France invaded Britain. The invasion not only changed many aspects of British life; it brought many French words into the language. Many of these French words had originally come from Latin.

Here are some examples of English words that have come from Latin:

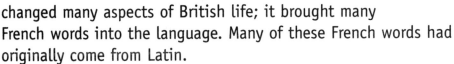

- words containing **c** [making a /s/ sound] such as **c**ell, **c**entre, **c**ity and medi**c**ine;

- words containing **g** [making a /j/ sound] such as **g**iant, a**g**ent, ima**g**ine and ori**g**inal

- words containing **ti, ci** or **ssi** [making a /sh/ sound] such as na**ti**on, offi**ci**al and commi**ssi**on.

Classical spelling patterns

Listed below are some of the more common Classical Greek and Latin spelling patterns in modern English.

Classical pattern	Meaning	Examples
ann or enn	year	annual, anniversary, bicentennial, millennium
arch	main, chief, ruling	archbishop, monarch, archetype
bio	life	biology, biography, bio-diversity
chron	time	chronometer, chronicle, synchronise
cycl	round	bicycle, cyclic, cyclone, encyclopedia
duc	lead	introduce, education, produce, conduct
dyna	power	dynamic, dynamo, dynasty
fact	make	factory, satisfaction, artefact
form	shape	formation, uniform, inform, formula
gram	written/drawn	diagram, grammar, program
hydr	water	hydraulic, dehydrated, hydro-electric
itis	disease	tonsillitis, arthritis
log	study	logic, astrology, technology
log	speak	apologize, dialogue
man	hand	manual, manage, manufacture
onym	name	anonymous, synonym, homonym
phone	sound	telephone, symphony
phys	nature	physical, physiology
poly	many	polyunsaturated, polygon
popul	people	population, popular, populous
psych	mind	psychology, psychic, psychiatrist
rupt	break	disrupt, rupture, interrupt, corrupt
scop	observe	microscope, horoscope, telescope
sign	mark	design, signature, sign, significant
stella	star	constellation, stellar
sy	together	symphony, sympathy, system, symmetry
tele	distant	telephone, television
tend	lean towards	attend, intend, pretend
vis	see	visible, vision, visit

Unique North American etymologies

North America shares a special history of word usage. From early settlement from Britain and France came new words to describe life in North America.

Eskimo

The word **Eskimo**, used to describe a group of people living in northern Canada, has a mixed origin. It is believed by some that it comes from the Cree word, **askimowew**, meaning 'he eats it raw', which describes the Eskimo diet of raw meat. Its spelling was later influenced by the early French Canadian explorers who then called the Eskimo, Eskimaux.

It is interesting to note that the word Eskimo was the term used by the Indians and French Canadian, and later the future population to describe the inhabitants of Northern Canada. However, the Eskimos did not use this term. They called themselves the **Innuit** (or **Inuit**), meaning 'mankind', which has since become the more widely acceptable term.

Cajun

Acadia is a former French settlement in Nova Scotia, Canada. Faced with increasing encroachment from British colonists in 1713, many of the Acadians settled in Louisiana, United States. The term **Cajun**, used to describe the Acadians, their lifestyle and cooking, comes from the word **Acadian**. Try saying Acadian ten times fast and you will see how this word got its start!

Teddy Bear

The term teddy bear is a fairly recent addition to the English language. It came about during a hunting expedition in the United States in 1902 when American President Theodore (or Teddy for short) Roosevelt refused to shoot a bear cub. Subsequently, toy manufacturers began producing stuffed bears, calling them "Teddy Bears".

Spelling strategies that work

What is a spelling strategy?

There are lots of strategies good spellers use to help them spell words correctly. You can use them too. A spelling strategy is any method you use to remember how to spell a word, or to work out the spelling of a word you don't know. There are thirteen strategies listed in this section. Some of them are useful for memorizing words (great for words you use frequently or for your school spelling lists). Other strategies help you attack new words and difficult words.

Strategies to help you remember how to spell a word

Strategy 1   Look, say, cover, write, check

Strategy 2   'Chunking' words — syllabification

Strategy 3   'Chunking' words — compound words and words within words

Strategy 4   'Chunking' words — letter groups

Strategy 5   Concentrating on the hard part — highlighting the difficult part of the word

Strategy 6   Memory helpers of 'mnemonics'

Strategies to work out the spelling of a word you don't know

Strategy 7   Use rules

Strategy 8   Use letter sounds/pronunciation

Strategy 9   Use knowledge of word history and meaning

Strategy 10 Use a dictionary

Strategy 11 Use a spell checker

Strategy 12 Try spelling the word! Does it look right?

Strategy 13 Ask someone

Once you become confident with one strategy, move on and try some others. You'll probably find some strategies will suit you better than others.

Strategies to help you remember how to spell a word

 Strategy 1 Look, say, cover, write, check

This strategy is a good way to help you memorize new words. Here is how it works.

| Look | Look carefully at the word. Look for patterns, double letters and small words inside the word. Highlight any tricky parts. |

Look Look carefully at the word. Look for patterns, double letters and small words inside the word. Highlight any tricky parts.

Say Say the word slowly as you look at it. Think about the sounds the word makes.

Cover Cover the word.

Write Write the word next to the original.

Check Check your spelling. If you have not spelled the word correctly, or you were not completely sure of the spelling, go through the process again.

Repeat **look, say, cover, write, check** regularly until you are sure that you can spell the word confidently.

Strategy 2 'Chunking' words — syllabification

EN VI RON MENT

'Chunking' words is a way of making words easier to spell by breaking them up into smaller parts — chunks. A special type of chunking is the chunking of sounds. Every word is made up of one or more sounds. Each chunk of sound is called a syllable. Breaking a word into syllables is a handy spelling strategy. Say the word slowly, and ask yourself which groups of letters make up each separate sound. Draw a line between each syllable. Look at this example using the word **environment**.

Say the word   *environment*

Mark the syllables   *en/vi/ron/ment*

Using lines to show the syllables of a word is a good way of learning how to spell longer or difficult words. Look at these examples. They have been marked to show their syllables.

One syllable words	Two syllable words	Three syllable words
cat	method [me/thod]	example [ex/am/ple]
farm	doctor [doc/tor]	museum [mu/se/um]
fruit	orange [o/range]	pineapple [pine/ap/ple]
through	maybe [may/be]	adventure [ad/ven/ture]
sphinx	homework [home/work]	portable [por/ta/ble]
calmed	rattle [rat/tle]	national [na/tio/nal]

Try it yourself...

Find the three syllable word in this sentence.

Look at the beautiful flower over there.

Now work out how many syllables there are in the following sentence.

There are many different coniferous and deciduous trees in North America.

Which words have more than two syllables?

There are rules about separating syllables in some special cases. Most syllables begin with a consonant.

cau/tion Ve/nus

If there are double letters, draw the line between the double letters.

let/ter   bot/tle

But when a base word (that's a word that stands as a word all by itself, like **miss** in **missing**) ends in a double letter, draw the line between the base word and the other syllables.

miss/ing add/i/tion

For a compound word, which is a word made up of two words, draw a line to separate the two base words.

foot/path   class/room

Strategy 3 'Chunking' words — compound words and words within words

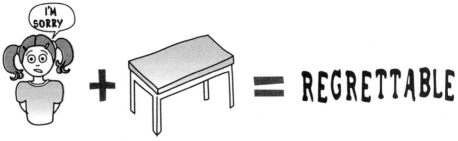

Here are some examples of how chunking **compound words** and **words within words** can make spelling easier.

Compound words

Compound words are longer words made up of two (or sometimes three) smaller words, such as:

throughout	through/out	everyone	every/one
raincoat	rain/coat	headache	head/ache
watermelon	water/melon	outside	out/side
grandfather	grand/father	bathroom	bath/room
sunrise	sun/rise	outdoorsman	out/doors/man

Words within words

Whole words — Some words are made up of smaller words but are not really compound words. Unlike true compound words, which are made by joining two words together, these words just happen to contain letters that make smaller words. This can make them easier to learn to spell. Here are some examples.

allowed	all/owed	beginning	beg/inning
cargoes	car/goes	father	fat/her
format	for/mat	manage	man/age
meant	me/ant	often	of/ten
regrettable	regret/table	together	to/get/her

Part words — Other words contain groups of letters that form at least one smaller word.

Finding smaller words within a word can help you learn how to spell them more easily. Here are some examples:

address	**add**ress or add**ress**
argument	argu**men**t
army	**arm**y or ar**my**
believe	bel**ie**ve
beneath	bene**ath**

business	**bus**iness or busi**ness**
clothes	clothes
colour	col**our**
environment	env**iron**ment
honest	hon**est**
sword	**sword**
theatre	**theatre** or thea**tre**

Now you try it. Find smaller words in the words of this passage.

The Children's Book Award is presented every year in June. The prize awarded is a medal that honors the author for an outstanding children's book. Most book stores, even small ones, stock the award-winning book.

 ## Strategy 4 'Chunking' words — letter groups

Many good spellers make spelling easier by breaking down words into smaller groups of letters. Instead of attacking the whole word, you can attack the word in smaller bits. Then it's just a matter of putting all the bits together.

Common letter combinations

Here are some examples:

-ight	light	right
-tion	nation	relation
-ing	string	singer
-ough	rough	tough
-tle	castle	nettle
-end	friend	send

Now you try it. Write three more words containing each of the common letter combinations in the above list.

Consonant blends

Here are some examples:

bl-	blend	black
br-	brown	break
-ch-	church	such
cr-	crush	creature
dr-	drip	drawer
fl-	flood	free
gl-	glance	glad
gr-	graph	degree
pl-	place	apply´
pr-	prince	probably
sc-	scatter	scene
scr-	scramble	describe
sh-	ship	sharp
shr-	shrill	shriek
sl-	slope	slippers
sp-	spill	speak
spl-	splint	splash
spr-	spring	spread
st-	steam	still
str-	strike	strap
sw-	swim	sword
th-	this	third
tr-	trip	tremendous
tw-	twelve	twist
wh-	who	whistle
wr-	write	wriggle

Now you try it. Write three more words containing each of the common letter combinations in the above list.

Vowel blends — including a vowel and -y

Here are some examples of vowel blends. Bear in mind that sometimes the letter **-y** is used as a vowel.

-ai-	rail	remain
-au-	taught	Paul
-ay	pay	today
-ea-	peace	tea
-ee-	seem	peer
-ei-	seize	receive
eu-	euchre	Europe
-ey	monkey	prey
-ie-	believe	relief
-oa-	roast	soar
-oe-	toe	poet
-oi	oil	spoil
-oo-	spool	poor
-ou-	about	devout
-oy	toy	deploy
-ue-	Sue	duet
-ui	ruin	build
-uy	buy	guy

Now you try it. Write three more words containing each of the vowel blends in the above list.

Now try finding the common letter combinations, consonant blends and vowel blends in the words of this passage.

The Royal Tyrrell Museum, located in the badlands of Alberta, Canada, is named after geologist Joseph Tyrrell. Tyrrell discovered many dinosaur fossils and skeletons in 1884. Today, the museum features many of the skeletons and fossils found near the area. In fact, more than eight hundred fossils are currently on display.

There are more examples of each of these in **Part 6, p 86.**

Strategy 5 Concentrating on the hard part
— highlighting the difficult part of the word

Words sometimes have a particular sequence of letters that cause some spellers problems. Different people find different parts of different words difficult. You can help yourself remember the difficult parts of words by using a highlighter to make the tricky section stand out. This will help it stick in your mind.

Here are some examples:

If you are anxious about spelling **anxious**, work out which letters cause a particular problem. Say you find the **–nxi–** confusing. Use a highlighter to mark those letters to help you remember them.

anxious

Or, if you find it necessary to look up **necessary** every time you want to spell it, once again work out which letters you find most difficult to remember. Highlight them with a highlighter.

necessary

Now you try. Which tricky parts of the words of this passage would you highlight?

The safety of ships in ports is the responsibility of the Harbour Master. A Harbour Master must have previously served as a ship's captain. Harbour Masters are helped by pilots, who board ships entering and leaving port to guide them through the port area and direct the tugs, which assist the ship to manoeuvre along the narrow channels.

Strategy 6 Memory helpers or 'mnemonics'

Many people remember how to spell tricky words by making up a phrase or rhyme to remind them of the correct spelling. The correct name for these memory helpers is **mnemonics** (pronounced ne-mon-icks). You can use mnemonics for words you have trouble spelling.

Mnemonics are particularly useful in remembering which **homonym** to use in which situation. Homonyms are words that look or sound the same, but have different meanings. (See **Part 5, p 55.**)

Look at these examples of common mnemonics.

⭐**A friend to the end** reminds us that the word **friend** ends with the letters **end**.

⭐**The Principal is my pal** reminds us that the **Principal** of a school ends with the letters **pal**.

A FRIEND TO THE END

THE PRINCIPAL IS MY PAL

⭐**Ice is a noun and so is practice** reminds us that the noun **practice** ends with the letters **ice** (tennis practice), while the word **practise** is the verb (I will **practise** my tennis).

⭐**A piece of pie** reminds us that the word **piece** (meaning 'part of something') begins with the letters **pie**.

A PIECE OF PIE

Some useful mnemonics

Word	Mnemonic	Comment
bear	a bear bit my ear	homonym: bear/bare
business	there is a bus in business	also: I am in business
cemetery	three e's are in the cemetery	confused with -ary ending
diary	a diary begins with 'I'	confused with dairy
environment	three n's in environment	middle n often omitted
government	two n's in government	first n often omitted
hear	hear with your ear	homonym: hear /here
island	an island is land	silent letter: s
loose	a loose tooth	confused with 'lose'
meat	animals eat meat	homonym: meat/meet
parallel	the middle l's are parallel	reminds you to include double l
sail	I ail when I sail	homonym: sail/sale
separate	a rat is separate	also: separate ends with rate
theatre	the, at, re	tricky spelling

You can make up your own mnemonics for words you find difficult. In fact the ones you make up yourself are often easier to remember than ones made up by other people.

Now you try. Make up mnemonics for some of these tricky words.

aloud	doctor	doesn't
flower	forty	necessary
steak	sugar	through
pneumonia	recommend	umbrella

Now make up mnemonics for some words you have trouble with.

Strategies to help you work out the spelling of a word you don't know

Strategy 7 Use rules

A spelling rule is a helpful guide to spelling words correctly. However, there are many exceptions to the rules and some words (especially words that have come from other languages) do not follow any of the common rules. Sometimes spelling rules are called spelling conventions.

A list of rules is given in **Part 4, p 41**.

I BEFORE E EXCEPT AFTER

Strategy 8 Use letter sounds/pronunciation

Many spelling mistakes occur because words are not pronounced correctly. Saying words correctly makes it easier to work out how to spell them. Here are some words that are commonly mispronounced, and so misspelled.

GOV...ERN...MENT

Antarctica	athlete	atomize	burglar
clothes	diamond	environment	February
government	known	library	nearly
particularly	picture	probably	recognize
sandwich	secretary	strength	stumble
temporary	tired	umbrella	Wednesday

Now you try. Practise saying the words in the list correctly. Think about how many syllables they contain (for example, **particularly** is a five syllable word, and so the spelling of **particurly**, which would have four syllables, is obviously not correct.)

Strategy 9 Use knowledge of word history and meaning

Some good spellers spell unknown words by using their knowledge of the history of words and word meanings. The history of words is called etymology. Knowledge of a word's root — the language it originally came from — can tell us a lot about how it is spelled. Some examples follow.

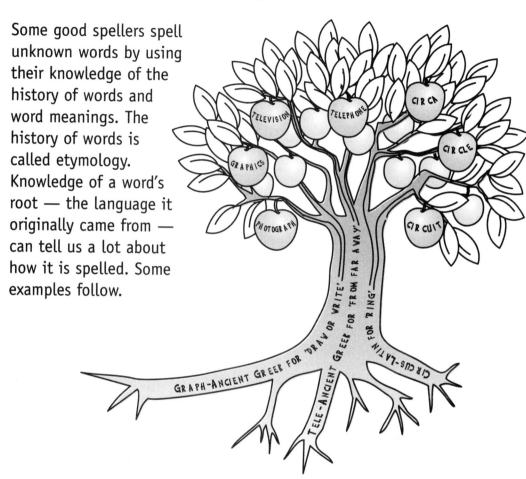

Word	Hint
centum	Latin for 'hundred', helps spell **cent**, **century**, **centenary** and **percent**.
circus	Latin for 'ring', helps spell **circle** and **circuit**.
tele	Ancient Greek for 'from far away' helps spell **telephone** (phone = to hear), **telegraph**, **teleport**, **television**.
graph	Ancient Greek for 'draw or write' helps spell **photograph**, **telegraph**, **calligraphy**, **graphics**.

Knowledge of words and word parts is called morphemic knowledge. For example, knowing that the word **knowledge** comes from the word **know** helps us remember its spelling, because **knowledge** starts with **know**.

Here are some other examples.

Word	Hint
leadership	means 'the skill of leading', and so begins with **lead**.
anxiety	means 'being anxious', and so begins with **anxi**.
doesn't	contraction of **does not**, and so begins with **does**.
environment	comes from **environ** (surrounding) plus **ment** (hence **nm**).
government	comes from **govern** (rule over) plus **ment** (hence **nm**).
prehistoric	means 'before recorded history', and so contains **hist**.
signature	means 'personal sign or mark', and so begins with **sign**.

Now you try.

Use a Dictionary of Etymology (or a good dictionary with word histories) to find the origins of these words. There are five words from each of these origins: French, Ancient Greek, Old English, Latin and First Nations languages.

acrobat	acute	aeronautics	alias	alligator
alphabet	baboon	beetle	brochure	chinook
circus	cricket	democracy	dizzy	dream
drench	echidna	eerie	emotion	encore
excite	igloo	kayak	muskeg	toboggan

⭐ Five words from First Nations languages. _____

_____

⭐ Five words of French origin. _____

_____

⭐ Five words of Old English origin. _____

_____

Five words of Latin origin. _____

_____

 Five words of Ancient Greek origin._____

_____

Strategy 10 Use a dictionary

I'M YOUR SPELLING FRIEND

Dictionaries are very useful spelling tools. Here are some hints on how to use a dictionary effectively.

On a piece of scrap paper, try writing the word you want to spell. Look up the word you have written. If it is in the dictionary, celebrate! You have spelled the word correctly. (Check the meaning, though, to make sure that the word is really the one you are after.)

If you cannot find your spelling in the dictionary, try spelling the word again. Use some other strategies such as chunking or mnemonics.

Always use a suitable dictionary, written for your age group. The small type and huge number of words found in adult dictionaries make it hard to find the word you want, and the definitions are likely to contain words which you may not understand.

Strategy 11 Use a spell checker

The spell check function of a word processing computer program checks each word in a document to see if there is an identical word in the program's dictionary. If a word is not stored in the program dictionary, it will come up as a spelling 'error'.

However, spell checkers do not check that the correct word has been used. It would not pick up a mistake such as 'He gave the men there coats' instead of 'He gave the men **their** coats'.

 The spell checker will not find typing errors which by chance result in a real word. For example, a spell checker will not tell you if you accidentally type **bat** instead of **bar**, and it will not find errors such as **bear** used instead of **bare**.

RUNNING SPELLCHECK NOW!

Most spell checkers allow you to build custom dictionaries of your own words such as names of people and places that do not appear in normal dictionaries. (Be careful though, if you are using someone else's computer. They may have added incorrectly spelled words to their customized dictionary.)

Good word processing software will allow you to choose spelling variations, so that words such as *color* for *colour* will be tagged. These tools help make spell checkers more helpful.

Remember, the fact is that, even though you have used a spell checker, you still have to proofread your work before you print it.

Now you try. Experiment with a spell checker to see how it works. Make some deliberate mistakes and see which words the spell checker suggests.

 ## Strategy 12 Try Spelling the Word! Does it look right?

This strategy is probably the most common way good spellers spell words they are not completely sure of. Most adults use this method, and if this does not work they will use a dictionary or a computer spell checker.

On a scrap of paper, try spelling a word. Think about the sounds the word makes. Are there any common prefixes or suffixes? A prefix is a group of letters added to the front of a word to add to, or change, its meaning. For example, add **im** to **polite** to form its opposite, **impolite**.

A suffix is a group of letters added to the end of a word to add to, or change, its meaning. For example, add **ful** to the noun **joy** to form the adjective **joyful**.

Are there common word-building elements such as **-ing** or **-ed**? Are there any sounds that are usually 'chunked' into certain letter patterns such as **-str**?

Once you have written the word, look at it. Ask yourself: 'Does it look right?' If it looks right, it probably is right! If you are not sure, use a dictionary.

The more times you see a word, the better you remember it. The secret is to read lots! The more you read, the easier it is to use the 'Does it look right?' method.

 ## Strategy 13 Ask someone

This strategy needs no explanation!

Spelling to rule

Spelling rules are helpful tools that can help us become better spellers. Spelling rules can help us spell accurately by giving guidelines on how to make plurals (more than one), how to add suffixes (such as **-ly** and **-ment**) and how to change the form of verbs (for example, by adding **-ing**).

Words that have come into English from other languages often keep that language's spelling rules and letter combinations. Many of the rules we have in English have come from other languages. A knowledge of word history (etymology) helps us follow the rules, because then we know which language the spelling rules have come from.

Here are some useful rules. You will probably discover that you already know and follow many of them!

How the rules work

If a word ends in -ch, add -es.

This rule applies to plural nouns and to changes in verb forms.

ONE LUNCH   **TWO LUNCHES**

Plural nouns

one lunch	two lunches
one batch	many batches
one coach	four coaches
one branch	many branches
one scratch	many scratches
one sandwich	six sandwiches
one match	a box of matches
one peach	a box of peaches

ONE PEACH

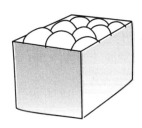

A BOX OF PEACHES

Exception:
If the -ch makes a /k/ sound, just add -s.
one monarch   two monarchs
one stomach   two stomachs

Verbs

Can you reach the top shelf?
Sarah easily reaches the top shelf.

Be careful! My cat may scratch you.
My cat often scratches our furniture.

They watch hockey every Saturday.
He watches hockey every Saturday.

If a word ends in -sh, add -es.

This rule applies to plural nouns and to changes in verb forms.

Plural nouns

one flash	five flash**es**
one bush	two bush**es**
one sash	many sash**es**
one wish	three wish**es**
one gash	three long gash**es**
one finish	many close finish**es**
one brush	three brush**es**
one blush	deep red blush**es**

ONE BLUSH

DEEP RED BLUSHES

Exception:
Don't be caught by fish!
    Remember: one **fish** ... two **fish**

Verbs

Do not rush your work.
Alicia often rush**es** her work.

I will wash the dog.
Mom usually wash**es** the dog.

My sisters never fish in the creek.
Dean never fish**es** in the creek.

43

If a word ends in -ss or -s, add -es.

This rule applies to plural nouns and to changes in verb forms.

Plural nouns

one bus	a fleet of buses
one gas	a mixture of gases
one octopus	eight octopuses
one mass	different masses
one address	a book of addresses

Verbs

It is easy to miss the ball.
Paul usually misses the ball.

Do you possess an encyclopedia?
The school possesses fifty computers.

Three buses pass the railway station.
One bus passes the railway station.

If a word ends in -o, add either -s or -es.

This rule applies to plural nouns and to changes in verb forms.

Add **-es** to the following words:

Plural nouns

one mosquito	a swarm of mosquitoes
one buffalo	a herd of buffaloes
one potato	a bag of potatoes
one volcano	three volcanoes
one mango	five juicy mangoes
one tomato	a box of tomatoes

ONE TOMATO   **TWO TOMATOES**

Verbs

I do my homework every week.
Nicholas do**es** his homework every week.

The sound will echo across the valley.
The sound echo**es** across the valley.

The chairperson can veto the decision.
The chairperson rarely veto**es** a decision.

Add **-s** to the following words:

one piano	three pianos
one cello	a pair of cellos
one soprano	my favourite sopranos
one solo	two solos
one concerto	Chopin's concertos
one radio	four radios
one video	two videos
one stereo	two stereos
one photo	an album of photos
one zero	a row of zeros
one folio	several folios
one taco	three crisp tacos
one zoo	all the nation's zoos

If a word ends in -x or -z, add –es.

This rule applies to plural nouns and to changes in verb forms.

Important:
If the **z** comes after a vowel, double the **z** before adding the **-es**.

Plural nouns

one six	three sixes
one tax	Federal taxes
one fox	a plague of foxes

A FOX

A PLAGUE OF FOXES

one waltz	two slow waltzes
one box	a pile of boxes
one quiz	three quizzes
one fez	three red fezzes (a flat-topped hat with a tassel)

Verbs

Chefs mix the ingredients well.
The chef mixes the ingredients well.

The Government will tax gasoline.
The Government taxes gasoline.

The detective will quiz the criminal.
My teacher quizzes us on our multiplication.

> If a word ends in a consonant and -y,
> change -y to -i and add -es

This rule applies to plural nouns and to changes in verb forms.

Plural nouns

one party	both part**ies**
one army	the allied arm**ies**
one canary	five canar**ies**
one library	all school librar**ies**
one factory	the town's main factor**ies**
one dictionary	a set of dictionar**ies**
one navy	all the world's nav**ies**
one butterfly	many butterfl**ies**

ONE CANARY   **FIVE CANARIES**

Verbs

Please carry my bag to the car.
The new bus carr**ies** forty-six people.

We will have to hurry or we will be late.
He always hurr**ies** to school.

I always try my best.
Kate tr**ies** to do her best.

Here are some examples.

Base word	Add -es	Add -ed	Add -ly	Add -able	Add -ness	Add -ment
carry	carries	carried				
cry	cries	cried				
vary	varies	varied		variable		
merry			merrily			merriment
happy			happily		happiness	

Helpful hint: To avoid having double i, always keep the final **-y** when adding **-ing**. For example:

try	trying	carry	carrying
vary	varying	spy	spying
bury	burying	satisfy	satisfying

Important:
Watch out for **skiing**, which does contain double **i**.

This rule applies to plural nouns and to changes in verb forms.

Plural nouns

one monkey   a cage full of monkeys

one railway   North America's railways

ONE KEY	A BUNCH OF KEYS
one highway	the state's highways
one chimney	a row of chimneys
one key	a bunch of keys
one boy	too many boys
one turkey	a farmyard of turkeys
one display	several great displays

Verbs

Base word	Add -s	Add -ed	Add -ing
play	plays	played	playing
employ	employs	employed	employing
enjoy	enjoys	enjoyed	enjoying
delay	delays	delayed	delaying
pay	pays	(paid)*	paying
buy	buys	(bought)*	buying

* Some verbs in the past tense change their form rather than adding **-ed**.

This rule also applies to adjectives. Adjectives are words that describe, or give more information about, a noun or pronoun.

Adjectives

Base word	Add -ful	Add -less	Add -ous
joy	joyful	joyless	joyous
play	playful		

Put i before e except after c.

ie words:

achieve	believe	brief	chief	field
fiend	grief	grieve	niece	piece
priest	relief	relieve	shield	shriek
siege	thief	yield		

cei words:

ceiling	conceit	conceive	deceit	deceive
perceive	receipt	receive		

Exceptions:
Watch out for these:

seize	weir	weird	protein	caffeine
codeine	Neil	Sheila	Keith	Reid

If a word ends in a silent -e, drop the -e to add a suffix beginning with a vowel (including -y).

Base word	Add **-ed**	Add **-ing**	Add **-y**	Add **-ous**	Add **-al**	Add **-ion**
use	used	using				
admire	admired	admiring				
scare	scared	scaring	scary			
nerve			nervy	nervous		
culture	cultured				cultural	
fuse	fused	fusing				fusion

Important:
Keep the final **-e** when adding a suffix beginning with a consonant.

ADMIRING   **ADMIR**ED

Base word	Add **-ly**	Add **-ful**	Add **-less**	Add **-ness**	Add **-ty**	Add **-some**
sore	sorely			soreness		
loose	loosely			looseness		
safe	safely				safety	
lone	lonely					lonesome
care		careful	careless			
hope		hopeful	hopeless			
use		useful	useless			
noise			noiseless			

Important:
Do not drop the final **-e** when adding **-able** to words ending in **-ce** and **-ge** which have a soft sound.

notice	notic**eable**
manage	manag**eable**
change	chang**eable**
replace	replac**eable**
service	servic**eable**
trace	trac**eable**

If a word ends in a single vowel followed by a single consonant, double the consonant to add a suffix beginning with a vowel.

Base word	Add -ed	Add -ing	Add -er
bat	batted	batting	batter
travel	travelled	travelling	traveller
marvel	marvelled	marvelling	
commit	committed	committing	
control	controlled	controlling	controller

Base word	Add -ous	Add -al	Add -able
marvel	marvellous		
commit		committal	
control			controllable

Some special plurals

In most cases you can form plurals of nouns ending in -f or -fe, by changing the -f, or -fe, to -v and adding -es.

one calf	many calves
one leaf	all the tree's leaves
one life	nine lives
one elf	many elves
one thief	a gang of thieves
one shelf	a set of shelves
one wolf	a pack of wolves
one loaf	five loaves

ONE ELF

MANY ELVES

Look out for these exceptions. Study them carefully.

chiefs   roofs   handkerchiefs   cliffs   reefs

Some words ending in **-f** can have either plural.

one wharf	two wharf**s** or two whar**ves**
one hoof	four hoof**s** or four hoo**ves**

Some plurals are made by changing some of the letters of the base word, or by adding an unusual suffix.

one woman	two women
one man	forty men
one child	a class of children
one person	three people
one tooth	a set of false teeth
one goose	a gaggle of geese
one foot	two left feet
one die	a pair of dice
one mouse	three blind mice
one louse	covered in lice
one cactus	seven cacti
one fungus	a number of fungi
a phenomenon	strange phenomena
a medium	different media
one sphinx	two sphinges
one cherub	a host of cherubim
one ox	a herd of oxen
one crisis	too many crises

ONE GOOSE

A GAGGLE OF GEESE

Some nouns exist only as plurals.

one fish	a school of fish
one deer	a herd of deer
one salmon	four salmon
one sheep	a mob of sheep
one elk	five elk
one innings	two innings
one pair of scissors	thirty pairs of scissors
one pair of tweezers	two pairs of tweezers
one pair of trousers	three pairs of trousers
one pair of pants	many pairs of pants

Spelling fiends

There are some words that many people (even adults) find hard to spell. Some are easily confused with other words, some have unusual letter combinations, and some are misspelled because they are often mispronounced.

100 common spelling fiends

absence	accommodation	ache	address
again	allowed	among	answer
babies	beautiful	beginning	believe
blue	break	built	business
busy	buy	can't	choose
clothes	color*	coming	could
country	dear	doctor	does
doesn't	don't	early	easy
enough	environment	every	February
forty	friend	government	guess
half	having	hear	heard
here	hoping	hour	instead
knew	library	loose	lose
many	meant	minute	much
often	once	piece	practice
principal	probably	quiet	safety

* The spelling of **color** varies by where you live. In Canada, **color** can be spelled **color**, with an 'or' ending, or **colour**, with an 'our' ending. In the United States, color is spelled with an 'or' ending. In this book, we spell **color** with an 'or' ending.

said	seems	separate	shoes
since	speech	straight	stretch
sugar	sure	tear	their
there	they	though	through
tired	tonight	too	trouble
Tuesday	two	used	wear
Wednesday	week	where	whether
which	whole	women	won't
would	write	writing	wrote

Use some of the spelling strategies in **Part 3** (such as mnemonics, chunking and 'look, say, cover, write, check') to help you conquer these spelling fiends.

Create your own personal spelling word list to write out your own personal spelling fiends.

Now read on, to learn about two special types of spelling fiends — **silent letters** and **homonyms**.

Silent letters

Over time, the way we pronounce words changes. A thousand years ago the word **knife** was pronounced **k-nife**. This was clumsy and hard to say, so over time people stopped sounding the separate **k**. However, the spelling of the word remained the same. The **k** became a silent letter.

Another example is the word **night**, which was once pronounced **nict**, with the **-gh-** making a k sound. Gradually the k sound disappeared, but again, the spelling of the word remained unchanged.

Some words with silent letters have come from other languages. For example, the word **hour**, pronounced **our**, comes from French, and the word **spaghetti**, pronounced **spa-get-ti** comes from Italian. Both contain a silent h because the **h** is not pronounced in these languages.

Here are some common words that contain silent letters.

Common silent letters

✪ Silent b

comb	crumb	debt
doubt	dumb	lamb
limb	numb	thumb

LAMB WITH A SILENT B

✪ Silent c

conscious	muscle	scene
science	scissors	

SCISSORS WITH A SILENT

✪ Silent d

friendship	grandfather	handkerchief
Wednesday	windmill	

(The d in these words is still sometimes pronounced, but it is becoming less common.)

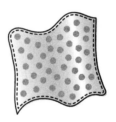

HANDKERCHIEF WITH A SILENT D

✪ Silent e

base	bite	hide
ice	large	life
mistake	name	owe
pale		

ICE WITH A SILENT E

GNOME WITH A SILENT G

⭐ Silent g

align	campaign	design
foreign	gnat	gnaw
gnome	reign	resign
sign		

VERANDAH WITH A SILENT H

⭐ Silent h

exhibit	ghost	ghoul
honest	honour	hour
rhyme	rhythm	spaghetti

KNOT WITH A SILENT K

⭐ Silent k

knee	kneel	knew
knife	knight	knit
knob	knock	knot

CALF WITH A SILENT L

⭐ Silent l

almond	calf	calm
chalk	could	folk
half	talk	walk

✪ Silent n

autumn	column	condemn
damn	hymn	

COLUMN WITH
A SILENT N

✪ Silent p

corps	coup	cupboard
pneumonia	psalm	psychiatrist
psychic	psychology	raspberry
receipt		

RASPBERRY WITH
A SILENT P

✪ Silent s

aisle	chassis	corps
debris	viscount	

VISCOUNT WITH A
SILENT S

✪ Silent t

ballet	bouquet	castle
debut	fasten	depot
listen	often	ricochet
whistle		

WHISTLE WITH
A SILENT T

✪ Silent u

guard	guess	guest
guide	guitar	

GUITAR WITH A SILENT U

✪ Silent w

answer	know	saw
sword	who	whole
wrap	wrestle	wrist

WRESTLE WITH A SILENT W

Homonyms

Homonyms are pairs of words that look or sound the same but have different meanings. 'Homo' means 'the same' and 'nym' means 'name' — homonym. So a homonym refers to two or more words, which either sound or are spelled the same, but have different meanings.

They can often be confusing, even for good spellers. There are two types of homonyms: **homographs** and **homophones**.

What is the difference between a homograph and a homophone? A close look at the two words will tell us.

'Graph' means 'write'   Homograph

'Phone' means 'sound'   Homophone

A **Homo** (same) + **Graph** (write) is a word that has the same spelling, but a different meaning, from another word. Sometimes homographs have different pronunciations.

Please **seal** the envelope.
The **seal** performed at the circus.

I have a **check** shirt.
I always **check** my work.

I will **wind** up the rope.
The cyclone brought a strong **wind**.

**THE CYCLONE BROUGHT
A STRONG** WIND

I WILL WIND
UP THE ROPE

A **Homo** (same) + **Phone** (sound) is a word with the same pronunciation, but a different meaning, from another word. Homophones often have different spellings.

I have **been** to the Opera House.
The **bean** plant covered the fence.

The referee was very **fair**.
We paid the bus **fare** to the driver.

**THE REFEREE
WAS VERY** FAIR

WE PAID THE BUS
FARE **TO THE DRIVER**

It is usually homophones that cause most trouble to spellers. Sometimes it is hard to remember which spelling fits which meaning. Many people use mnemonics to help them remember which word fits which meaning. For example, 'a piece of pie' reminds us that the word for a portion of something is spelled 'piece', not 'peace', because we link the word **pie** with the word **piece** and they share the first three letters. Some useful mnemonics are listed in **Part 3, p. 32.**

Study the following examples carefully. If in doubt, you can use this section to check that you are using the correct word, or you can look the word up in the dictionary.

Homophone	Meaning	Sentence
allowed	permitted	Emily is **allowed** to go to the party.
aloud	able to be heard	Lisa said the poem **aloud** to the assembly.
ate	consumed food	Tom **ate** fifteen hamburgers.
eight	a number	He also had **eight** packets of chips.
bean	a vegetable	I ate one **bean**.
been	existed	Have you ever **been** to Perth?
blew	puffed out air	I **blew** out all the candles.
blue	a color	Mrs Franklin's new car is **blue**.
bough	branch of a tree	The large **bough** came down in the storm.
bow	bend at the waist	Common people should **bow** to the king.
bow	front of a boat	We sat in the **bow** of the speedboat.
brake	slow down	The driver will **brake** to stop the car.
break	smash into pieces	Be careful not to **break** the new dish.
buy	purchase	I will **buy** a new computer next year.
by	near	The house is **by** the creek.
cent	an amount of money	I owe Dad one **cent**.
scent	smell	I smell the **scent** of a skunk.
sent	posted by mail	I **sent** Nan a letter.
cereal	grain	Wheat is an important **cereal** crop.
serial	in a series	We watched the **serial** on TV.
check	examine	Please **check** your answers.
check	a pattern of crosses	Mr Chapman wore a **check** tie.
cheque or* check	method of payment	We gave the milkman a **cheque** (or check).
coarse	rough	The old blanket was very **coarse**.
course	direction	The captain set **course** for Hobart.

*In the United States it is spelled '**check**.' In Canada it is spelled '**cheque**' or '**check**.'

Homophone	Meaning	Sentence
dear	expensive	The game was too **dear** to buy.
dear	loved	The bracelet is very **dear** to me.
deer	an animal	The **deer** leapt over the fence.
fair	light coloured	Ben has **fair** hair.
fair	follows the rules	The umpire made a **fair** decision.
fair	a market	I bought candy floss at the **fair**.
fare	money for travel	The **fare** for the trip to Montreal was ten dollars.
flour	ground wheat	The recipe used three cups of **flour**.
flower	a bloom	A rose is a lovely **flower**.
for	in favour of, because	We went to town **for** the carnival
four	a number	Mrs Franklin's new car has **four** doors.
grate	a grid	The storm water flowed through the **grate**.
great	very large	A **great** crowd gathered for the soccer match.
guessed	estimated	I **guessed** that the answer was one.
guest	visitor	The **guest** stayed in the spare room.
heal	cure	My cut will **heal** in time.
heel	back of foot	I have a sore **heel**.
heard	sensed by ear	We **heard** the bell.
herd	group of cattle	The **herd** slowly walked to the dairy.
hear	sense by ear	Can you **hear** the crickets?
here	this place	**Here** is where you left the bat.
hole	opening	The mouse crept through the **hole** in the wall.
whole	entire	The **whole** class performed in the play.
hour	sixty minutes	I waited for an **hour**.
our	belonging to us	That is **our** classroom.

Homophone	Meaning	Sentence
its	belonging to it	The dog returned to **its** kennel.
it's	it is (contraction)	'It's a hot day,' said Mr Hall.
knew	had knowledge of	Marnie **knew** the seven times table.
new	recent	I read the **new** book.
knot	a fastening	I tied a double **knot** in my shoelaces.
not	refusal	You may **not** sleep in the tent.
know	have knowledge of	Do you **know** the name of the Mayor?
no	refusal, none	I made **no** mistakes in the spelling test.
lead	a heavy metal	The sinker is made of **lead**.
led	pulled along	Casey **led** the horse to the water hole.
made	constructed	Mom and I **made** a treehouse.
maid	female servant	The **maid** served breakfast to the guests.
meat	animal flesh	Lamb is my favourite type of **meat**.
meet	be introduced to	I will **meet** the new principal.
missed	avoided	I **missed** the target.
mist	fog	The **mist** blanketed the forest.
pair	two	I have a new **pair** of shoes.
pear	a fruit	My favourite fruit is the **pear**.
passed	went by (verb)	The soldiers **passed** the memorial.
past	finished (adjective)	Those times are **past**.
peace	absence of war	People welcomed **peace** in 1945.
piece	a part	I ate a **piece** of apple for recess.
practice	action, routine (noun)	Kathryn is at hockey **practice**.
practise	to train (verb)	Always **practise** truthfulness and honesty.

Homophone	Meaning	Sentence
principal	main, leader	Mr Bradman, the **principal**, is his baseball team's **principal** run scorer.
principle	guiding belief	I believe in the **principle** of democracy.
rain	water from clouds	We received a good fall of **rain**.
reign	a period of rule	King Jason's **reign** began in 1842.
rein	controls a horse	One pull on the **rein** stopped the horse.
read	understood written words	Aaron **read** the story.
red	a color	The book had a **red** cover.
right	direction	The car turned **right** at Brush Road.
right	correct	I got all the math problems **right**.
right	privilege, due	We all have the **right** to feel safe at school.
write	mark words	Please **write** a report on the excursion.
sail	travel by boat	The boat will **sail** tomorrow morning.
sale	can be bought	The trampoline is for **sale**.
sew	stitch cloth	It is easy to **sew** a library bag.
so	a certain amount	Do not walk **so** fast.
sow	plant seeds	It is best to **sow** grass seed in spring.
sight	vision	The robber ducked out of **sight**.
site	location	The new school will be built on a **site** by the lake.
stake	wooden pole	The tomato plant was held up with a **stake**.
steak	meat from a cow	We all ate fillet **steak** at the restaurant.
tail	rear end	The cat's **tail** was stuck in the door.
tale	a story	The teacher told us a scary **tale**.

Homophone	Meaning	Sentence
their	belonging to them	That is **their** house.
there	that place	Put the scissors over **there**.
threw	tossed	Kate **threw** the ball to the first baseman.
through	via	Melissa ran **through** the classroom door.
to	in the direction of	Jack went **to** Europe for Christmas.
too	also	His sister Jill went **too**.
two	a number	They stayed for **two** weeks.
way	method or route	Do you know the **way** to the Beach?
weigh	find the weight	Please **weigh** the beans.
weak	lacking strength	He was too **weak** to lift the elephant.
week	seven days	He kept trying to lift it for a whole **week**.
whose	which person's	**Whose** book is this?
who's	who is (contraction)	That is the boy **who's** going to clean the sink.

Some useful word lists

The words in this chapter are listed in three ways. The first section is made up of lists of words you may need to spell while studying certain themes or topics at school. The second section gives examples of words containing common letter patterns. These lists will be valuable tools to help you find out how to spell the words you need to write.

At the end of this chapter, there are several techniques you can use on your own to improve your spelling skills.

Theme lists

😃 Agriculture

boundary	calves	cultivation
dairying	drought	farmer
farming	farrow	fertilizer
grazing	harvest	livestock
paddock	plantation	plough
property	ranch	refinery
shearing	sheep	soy
sugar	wheat	winery

☻ Ancient civilizations

Acropolis	aqueduct	Athens
Babylon	chariot	Colosseum
column	Egyptians	gladiators
Greeks	Incas	Maya
mummies	Olympia	papyrus
Parthenon	Pharaohs	pyramids
Romans	sarcophagus	slaves
Sparta	Sumerians	statues
Tutankhamen		

☻ Art and craft

abstract	art	artist
bronze	brush	canvas
composition	enamelling	frame
glassblowing	glaze	jewellery
landscape	macramé	masterpiece
metalwork	painting	
perspective	porcelain	
portrait	pottery	
sculpture	sketch	
tone	woodwork	

☻ Birds and animals

alligator	bear	beaver
blackbird	blue jay	bobcat
caribou	chipmunk	deer

Birds and animals continued ...

dove	duck	eagle
elk	fox	goat
goose	groundhog	hummingbird
kingfisher	otter	owl
porcupine	skunk	squirrel
weasel	wolf	

😊 Careers

accountant	actor	architect
apprentice	builder	carpenter
chef	cleaner	clerk
dentist	doctor	electrician
engineer	farmer	journalist
manager	mechanic	miner
nurse	optometrist	painter
	photographer	physiotherapist
	plumber	sailor
	teacher	technician
	scientist	secretary
	veterinarian	

😊 Colors

auburn	azure	black
blue	bronze	brown

Colors continued ...

cream	emerald	green
gold	indigo	lemon
lilac	mauve	olive
orange	pink	purple
red	scarlet	silver
turquoise	violet	white
yellow		

☺ Computers

byte	CD-ROM	computer
copy	drive	email
edit	floppy disk	gigabyte
hard disk	install	Internet
keyboard	kilobyte	load
megabyte	memory	modem
monitor	mouse	paste
program	RAM	save
scanner	shut down	start up

☺ Continental drift

active	aftershock	collapse
collide	crater	dormant
drift	earthquakes	
epicentre	erupt	
eruption	extinct	

Continental drift continued ...

fault	Himalayas	Krakatoa
landslide	lava	magma
molten	mountain	plate
seismograph	subduction	volcanoes

☺ Countries

Afghanistan	Argentina	
Austria	Australia	
Belgium	Bosnia-Herzegovina	
Brazil	Canada	Chile
China	Croatia	Egypt
England	Finland	France
Germany	Greece	Holland
India	Indonesia	Iran
Iraq	Ireland	Israel
Italy	Jamaica	Kenya
Korea	Lebanon	Malaysia
Mexico	New Zealand	Nigeria
Norway	Pakistan	Papua New Guinea
Peru	Philippines	Portugal
Russia	Saudi Arabia	Scotland
Serbia	Spain	South Africa
Sweden	Switzerland	Thailand
Turkey	United States	Uruguay
Vietnam	Wales	Yugoslavia

☺ Dinosaurs

allosaurus	ankylosaurus	apatosaurus
armoured	brachiosaurus	carnivorous
corythosaurus	deinonychus	diplodocus
extinct	herbivorous	iguanodon
lizards	muttaburrasaurus	omnivorous
stegosaurus	triceratops	tyrannosaurus

☺ Disasters

airplane	aftershock	ambulance
blaze	brigade	collapse
crater	cyclone	debris
devastation	drought	duststorm
earthquake	emergency	epicentre
eruption	evacuation	extinguish
forest fire	flood	fuel
hurricane	ice storm	landslide
lava	levee	mining
molten	railway	rescue
safety	sandbags	shipwreck
thunderstorm	tornado	torrential
tremor	typhoon	
volcano	volunteer	
vulcanologist	warning	

😊 Environment

biodegradable	disposal	ecology
effluent	environment	food chain
forests	future	garbage
global	green	habitat
heritage	natural	nature
ozone layer	pesticides	
pollution	preservation	
protect	protection	
rainforest	recycle	
rubbish	waste	

😊 Fantasy

abracadabra	apparition	automaton
castle	disappear	Dracula
dragon	eerie	fantastic
Frankenstein	ghost	haunted
horror	imagination	mysterious
phantom	potion	supernatural
superstition	unbelievable	vampire
vanished	weird	werewolf
zombie		

☺ Food

appetite	apple	apricot
avocado	bakery	banana
beef	beverage	biscuit
bread	breakfast	broccoli
butcher	butter	canteen
cauliflower	cereal	cheese
chocolate	citrus	cocoa
coconut	coffee	cucumber
delicious	diet	digestion
dinner	drink	dough
energy	filling	flavor
flour	fresh	frozen
fruit	frying	grapefruit
grapes	hamburger	harvest
hunger	hungry	ingredients
juice	kabobs	lamb
lemonade	loaf	loaves
lunch	mandarin	mango
margarine	meal	meat
menu	milk	nectar
orange	orchard	passion fruit
pear	peach	pita
pineapple	pizza	
plum	pork	
potatoes	prepare	

Food continued ...

preserved	pumpkin	rice
sandwich	sausages	sour
spinach	steak	strawberries
swallow	tacos	taste
tea	texture	thirst
toast	tofu	variety
veal	water	watermelon
wholewheat	yeast	zucchini

Government

act	alderman	attorney general
backbenchers	bill	budget
cabinet	chamber	coalition
councillor	defence	democrat
education	election	electorate
federal	foreign affairs	governor
governor general	health	immigration
independent	law	liberal
local	mayor	member
minister	national	opposition
parliament	party	planning
preferences	preferential	president
prime minister	quorum	recess
representatives	republican	senate
social security	speaker	state
taxes	treasurer	vote

History

abolition	Acadia	American
civil rights	colonization	Revolution
commonwealth	Confederation	constitution
Declaration of Independence	Depression	desegregation
	emancipists	exploration
explorers	fur trade	gold rush
New France	Puritans	railway
rebellion	settler	slavery

Human body and its ailments

ankle	appendix	arthritis
asthma	body	bones
breast	bronchitis	bruise
cancer	chest	chickenpox
cough	diarrhoea	disease
elbow	eyes	feet
finger	forehead	fracture
gastric	glands	hands
headache	heart	hiccup
infection	intestine	kidney
knee	ligament	limb
liver	measles	muscle
nausea	organ	rheumatism
rubella	shoulder	skeleton

Human body and its ailments continued …

stomach	thigh	thumb
throat	wrist	tonsils

😊 Industry

automobiles	beef	coal
communication	cotton	dairy farming
electronics	fishing	gas
gold	lead	mining
oil	pork	sheep
shipbuilding	silver	steel
timber	tourism	transport
uranium	wheat	
wine	wool	

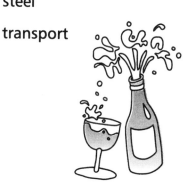

😊 Math

capacity	centigrade	centimetre
cylinder	decimal	division
eight	fifth	first
fourth	fraction	hexagon
hexagonal	inches	kilogram
kilometre	measurement	metre
millimetre	million	multiplication
ninth	numerical	octagon

Math continued ...

octagonal	parallelogram	pentagon
percentage	perimeter	prism
pyramid	rectangle	rectangular
rhombus	sphere	square
second	seventh	sixth
subtraction	temperature	thousand
tonne	trapezium	tenth
third	triangle	triangular
unit	volume	width
yard	zero	

Media

advertisement	articles	camera
channel	commentary	commercial
daily	editor	editorial
frequency	international	internet
interview	local	magazine
modem	national	network
newspaper	program	radio
studio	television	transmission
video		

Oceans

albatross	aqualung	beach
breakers	channel	cliffs
coast	coastline	coral
crustacean	currents	depth
diver	dolphin	fish
gulf	harpoon	headland
horizon	island	marine
nautical	navigation	ocean
oceanographer	plankton	rock
platform	sailing	sailor
sandbar	seagulls	seal
shallow	shark	shells
shipping	sonar	storm
strait	submarine	submerged
surf	surface	surfing
swell	tide	trawler
vessel	wave	whale	wreck

Performing arts

amateur	audience	ballad
ballerina	ballet	cast
chord	choreographer	chorus
classical	composer	concert
conductor	costumes	curtain
dance	drama	duet
entertainment	guitar	instruments

Performing arts continued ...

movement	music	narrator
opera	orchestra	piano
percussion	performance	pirouette
pitch	poetry	positions
production	professional	reggae
rehearsal	rhythm	role
scenery	stage	
theatre	traditional	
verse	violin	
waltz	xylophone	yodel

Places

Alabama	Alberta	Atlanta
Baltimore	Boston	British Columbia
California	Chicago	Florida
Grand Canyon	Great Lakes	Halifax
Lake Huron	Las Vegas	Los Angeles
Manitoba	Montreal	New York
Niagara Falls	Nevada	Ontario
Ottawa	Palm Springs	Prince Edward Island
Quebec	San Francisco	
Texas	Toronto	Vancouver
Victoria	Washington	Winnipeg

Plants

alfalfa

azalea

begonia

chrysanthemum

crocus

daffodil

dahlia

daisy

delphinium

gladiolus

heather

hyacinth

iris

lavender

lily

peony

poppy

marigold

narcissus

rhododendron

rose

snowdrops

sunflower

trillium

tulip

zinnia

Prehistory

amber

ancestors

anthropologist

archaeologist

Bronze Age

cavemen

dinosaurs

evidence

evolution

fire

flint

footprints

fossil

hunters

implements

imprint

Iron Age

mammoths

palaeontology

prehistoric

preserved

tribe

troglodyte

skeleton

Stone Age

☺ Relatives and friends

aunt	acquaintance	brother
cousin	daughter	descendent
divorce	family	father
friend	grandmother	grandfather
guardian	husband	mother
niece	neighbor	
nephew	person	
people	relation	
sibling	sister	
son	stepfather	
stepmother	stranger	
uncle	wife	

☺ Senses

hearing	sight	smell	taste	touch
acoustics	cornea	aroma	bitter	feel
audible	eyes	bouquet	flavor	manipulate
decibels	focus	exhale	hungry	rough
ears	lens	fragrance	recipe	sensation
noise	observe	inhale	salty	skin
pitch	perspective	nostrils	savory	smooth
tone	retina	odor	sour	tactile
voice	view	pungent	sweet	tangible
volume	vision	scent	tasty	texture

☺ Space

Apollo	Armstrong	asteroid
astronaut	astronomy	aurora
binary	black hole	capsule
comet	constellation	crater
crescent	Earth	eclipse
exploration	Gagarin	galaxy
gravitation	gravity	Halley's Comet
Jupiter	launch	light year
lunar	Mars	Mercury
meteor	meteorite	Milky Way
module	nebula	Neptune
observatory	planets	Pluto
pulsar	radiation	re-entry
rocket	Saturn	solar system
space shuttle	space station	telescope
Titan	universe	Uranus
Venus	weightlessness	

😊 Sports and games

archery	athlete	athletics
badminton	baseball	basketball
breaststroke	butterfly	carnival
champion	chess	competitors
cricket	cross-country	darts
decathlon	events	final
football	freestyle	goal
golf	handball	hockey
hopscotch	hurdles	javelin
judge	long distance	marathon
marbles	netball	Olympic
racquet	relay	ribbon
rugby	soccer	running
shot put	stadium	softball
sprint	team	tennis
swimming	volleyball	weightlifting
wrestling	water polo	

😊 Time

after	afternoon	April
August	autumn	before
centenary	century	clock
day	decade	December
digital	during	evening
February	Friday	hour

January	July	June
last	March	May
millennium	minute	Monday
month	morning	next
night	November	October
Saturday	second	September
spring	summer	Sunday
sundial	Thursday	today
tomorrow	Tuesday	Wednesday
week	winter	year
yesterday	zero hour	

Transportation

accident	airplanes	asphalt
automatic	automobile	avenue
bicycle	buses	boulevard
cabin	carriage	cockpit
control	conductor	cruise
cyclist	derailment	destination
engine	express	expressway
freeway	freight	gears
handlebars	highway	intersection
licence	locomotive	luggage
motorcycle	navigation	passenger
pedal	pedestrian	pressure

Transportation continued

registration	road	route
schedule	street	ticket
timetable	tire	traffic
train	transportation	tread
undercarriage	wheel	yacht

☺ Water

boil	bore	creek
dissolve	downstream	drainage
estuary	evaporate	float
flow	fluid	freeze
irrigation	ocean	outlet
reservoir	river	salinity
steam	stream	swamp
tributary	trickle	upstream
vapour	wade	watershed

☺ Weather

atmosphere	barometer	bureau
change	chinook	cyclone
drizzle	flood	forecast
front	frost	hail
humidity	hurricane	icicle
isobars	overcast	
ozone layer	rain	
satellite	sleet	snow
storm	temperature	thunderstorm

Word family lists

Common letter combinations

 -able

agreeable	allowable	available	advisable
acceptable	believable	consolable	comfortable
debatable	favorable	inflammable	lovable
movable	notable	portable	readable
regrettable	reliable	unstable	variable

 -ance

attendance	acceptance	admittance	appearance
defiance	disturbance	entrance	guidance
grievance	hindrance	ignorance	insurance
reliance	repentance	vengeance	

 -ant

assistant	buoyant	distant	elephant
extravagant	fragrant	ignorant	lubricant
merchant	pleasant	sergeant	tenant
tyrant	truant	vacant	

 -ary

boundary	burglary	diary	dictionary
hereditary	judiciary	library	legendary
necessary	ordinary	salary	sanctuary
secretary	solitary	stationary	summary
temporary	vocabulary	voluntary	

⭐ -eable

changeable	manageable	noticeable	peaceable
replaceable			

⭐ -ence

absence	audience	commence	conscience
difference	essence	defence	influence
negligence	obedience	preference	reference
science	sentence	violence	

⭐ -ent

adherent	agent	ancient	client
continent	confident	equivalent	evident
fluent	innocent	obedient	patient
repellent	resident	recent	sufficient
torrent	talent	urgent	violent

⭐ -eous

advantageous	bounteous	courteous	courageous
gorgeous	hideous	homogeneous	instantaneous
miscellaneous	nauseous	outrageous	piteous
righteous	simultaneous	spontaneous	

⭐ -er

adviser	barrister	believer	builder
character	convener	composer	disaster
diver	driver	father	invader

interpreter	minister	mother	murderer
officer	prisoner	passenger	painter
purchaser	teacher	transfer	traveller
waiter			

⭐ -ery

archery	bakery	cemetery	discovery
flattery	forgery	grocery	jewellery
machinery	misery	mockery	mystery
scenery	slippery	treachery	

⭐ -ful

awful	beautiful	careful	dutiful
faithful	fanciful	fearful	graceful
hateful	pitiful	plentiful	skillful
useful	watchful	wonderful	

⭐ -ible

accessible	admissible	audible	credible
compatible	combustible	edible	flexible
forcible	intelligible	invincible	permissible
responsible	sensible	tangible	

⭐ -ice

advice	crevice	device	entice
justice	lattice	notice	practice
service	suffice		

✪ -ight

alight	almighty	blight	bright
fight	flight	fright	height
light	might	mighty	night
plight	right	sight	slight
tight			

✪ -ing

bring	cling	cringe	dinghy
fling	hinge	jingle	king
mingle	ring	sing	singe
single	sling	spring	sting
string	tingle	wing	wring

✪ -ise

advertise	advise	arise	comprise
despise	devise	disguise	enterprise
franchise	surmise	surprise	

✪ -ious

audacious	curious	copious	dubious
gracious	laborious	noxious	obvious
spacious	studious		

✪ -ize

apologize	baptize	fantasize	memorize
prize	realize	size	tantalize
theorize			

-or

actor	ancestor	anchor	author
creator	doctor	debtor	horror
inspector	inventor	razor	sailor
tailor	traitor	vendor	

-ory

accessory	category	compulsory	cursory
inventory	lavatory	preparatory	promontory
transitory	victory		

-ough

although	bough	cough	enough
dough	plough	rough	slough
though	thorough	through	trough

-ought

bought	fought	nought	ought
sought			

-ous

arduous	disastrous	enormous	fabulous
grievous	nervous	poisonous	ridiculous
venomous	villainous		

-sion

accession	commission	decision	discussion
exclusion	expulsion	extension	expression
explosion	impression		

-tion

affection	attention	auction	communication
connection	correction	conversation	deduction
description	destruction	direction	exhaustion
explanation	exposition	information	instruction
invitation	nation	position	prevention
relation	revolution	sensation	situation
station			

 -tle

battle	bottle	brittle	bustle
castle	kettle	little	nettle
prattle	rustle	settle	trestle
turtle	whittle		

Consonant blends

 bl-

black	blackberry	blade	blame
blanket	blast	blaze	bleach
bleed	blend	bless	blew
blind	block	blood	bloom
blossom	blow	blue	blunt

 br-

brake	brain	branch	brass
brave	bread	break	breakfast

breath	breathe	breeze	brick
bridge	bright	bring	broad
broke	brooch	broom	brought
brother	brown	bruise	brush

⭐ ch-

chain	chair	chalk	champion
chance	change	chapter	charred
character	charge	chase	chatter
cheap	cheat	check	cheek
cheer	cheese	chemical	chemist
cheque	chest	chew	chicken
chief	child	children	chimney
chin	chip	chocolate	choice
choose	Christmas	church	

⭐ cr-

crab	crack	cradle	craft
crash	crawl	creak	cream
creature	credit	creek	creeper
crept	crew	cricket	crime
criminal	crocodile	crop	cross
crowd	crown	cruel	crush
crystal			

⭐ dr-

dragon	drain	drama	draw
drawer	dreadful	dream	dreary

dress	drew	dried	drier
drill	drink	drip	drive
drown	drum	dry	

⭐ fl-

flag	flair	flame	flan
flannel	flash	flee	fleet
flesh	flew	flight	float
flock	flood	floor	flour
flow	flower	flung	fly

⭐ fr-

fraction	frame	frantic	free
frequent	fresh	friend	fright
fringe	from	fruit	frog
front	frost	fry	

⭐ gl-

glad	glance	glass	gleam
glitter	globe	gloom	glorious
glory	glove		

⭐ -gr-

degree	grab	grace	gradual
grain	grand	grandfather	grandmother
graph	grasp	grass	grave
gravel	graze	great	greed

green	greet	grey	grip
groan	ground	group	grow
growth			

⭐ ph-

| phone | photo | photocopier | photograph |
| physical | | | |

⭐ -pl-

apply	place	plain	plan
plane	plank	plate	play
playful	playground	plead	pleasant
please	pleasure	plenty	plot
plough	plug	plunge	plunk

⭐ pr-

practical	practice	practise	pram
pray	prepare	present	president
press	pressure	pretend	pretty
previous	prey	price	prince
princess	principal	principle	print
prism	prison	private	prize
probable	probably	problem	procedure
procession	procure	produce	product
profit	program	progress	project
promise	proper	property	prove

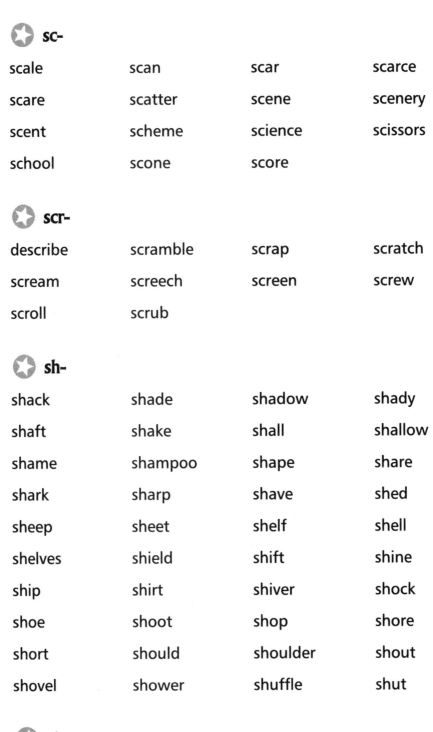

✪ sc-

scale	scan	scar	scarce
scare	scatter	scene	scenery
scent	scheme	science	scissors
school	scone	score	

✪ scr-

describe	scramble	scrap	scratch
scream	screech	screen	screw
scroll	scrub		

✪ sh-

shack	shade	shadow	shady
shaft	shake	shall	shallow
shame	shampoo	shape	share
shark	sharp	shave	shed
sheep	sheet	shelf	shell
shelves	shield	shift	shine
ship	shirt	shiver	shock
shoe	shoot	shop	shore
short	should	shoulder	shout
shovel	shower	shuffle	shut

✪ shr-

shrill	shriek	shrimp	shrivelled
shrub			

sk-

ask	basket	desk	mask
risk	skate	skater	skeleton
sketch	ski	skill	skillful
skim	skin	skip	skipping
skirt	sky	task	tusk

 sl-

slam	slant	slap	slate
slats	sleep	sleet	slept
slid	slide	slight	slime
slimy	slink	slip	slippers
slippery	slope	slow	slug

 sm-

smack	small	smart	smash
smell	smile	smoke	smoky
smooth	smuggler		

⭐ **sn-**

snail	snake	snap	snarl
snatch	sneeze	sniff	snip
snoop	snow		

⭐ **sp-**

space	spare	spark	speak
special	spectacle	speech	speed
spell	spend	spices	spider

| spill | spin | spirit | spoil |
| spoke | spoon | sport | spot |

⭐ spl-

display	splash	splatter	splay
spleen	splendid	splendor	splice
splint	split		

⭐ spr-

sprain	sprang	spray	spread
spring	sprinkle	sprint	sprite
sprocket	sprout		

⭐ squ-

squabble	squad	squall	square
squash	squeal	squeeze	squid
squiggle	squirrel		

⭐ st-

stable	stack	staff	stage
stain	stairs	stake	stalk
stall	stamp	stand	standard
star	stare	start	startle
state	statement	stationary	stationery
stay	steady	steak	steal
stealthy	steam	steel	steep
steer	stem	stepping	stick

sticky	stiff	still	sting
stitch	stock	stocking	stole
stomach	stone	stony	stood
stool	stop	stopped	storage
store	storm	story	stove
study	stump	stung	

✪ str-

destroy	instruct	mistreat	strange
stranger	strap	stream	street
strength	stretch	strike	string
strip	stripe	stroke	stroll
strong	struck	structure	struggle

✪ sw-

swallow	swam	swamp	sway
swear	sweat	sweep	sweet
swell	swift	swim	swing
switch	swoop	sword	

✪ th-

thank	their	there	thermometer
thick	thief	think	this
third	thirteen	thirty	those
thought	thousand	threw	throat
through	throw	thumb	Thursday

⭐ tr-

trace	track	traffic	tragedy
tragic	trail	train	tramp
transfer	transport	trapped	travel
traveller	tray	treasure	treat
tree	tremble	tremendous	trial
tribe	trick	tried	tries
trip	trolley	troops	tropical
trot	trouble	trough	trousers
truck	true	trunk	trust
truth	truthful	try	trying

⭐ tw-

twelve	twelfth	twentieth	twenty
twice	twig	twin	twine
twist	two		

⭐ wh-

whale	wharf	whatever	wheel
whenever	whether	which	while
whisk	whisker	whisper	whistle
white	who	whose	

⭐ wr-

wrap	wreck	wreckage	wrestle
wriggle	wrist	write	written
wrong	wrote		

Vowel blends (including a vowel and -y)

⭐ **-ai-**

again	afraid	available	brain
campaign	claim	complain	daily
detail	fail	faith	mail
plain	rail	remain	straight
trail	train	waist	wait

⭐ **-au-**

assault	author	autumn	audience
caught	cause	cautious	daughter
exhausted	fault	fraud	launch
naughty	onslaught	Paul	pause
raucous	sauce	slaughter	taught

⭐ **-ay-**

bay	bayonet	crayon	day
delay	essay	fray	may
mayonnaise	mayor	okay	play
pay	ray	rayon	say
stay	today	tray	way

⭐ **-ea-**

bear	bread	breakfast	each
eagle	ear	earth	Easter
feather	health	heaven	jealous
leather	measure	peace	pear
pleasant	rehearse	search	treasure

⭐ -ee-

been	beer	cheese	deep
feel	sixteen	flee	fleet
keep	need	peer	reef
screech	screen	seem	speech
steel	succeed	teeth	week

⭐ -ei-

beige	caffeine	ceiling	conceit
counterfeit	deceit	deceive	eight
neither	protein	receipt	seize
receive	rein	sheikh	surveillance
veil	vein	weird	

⭐ eu-

eucalyptus	eulogy	euphemism	Eureka

⭐ -ey

alley	attorney	chimney	donkey
galley	hockey	honey	jersey
jockey	journey	key	kidney
medley	money	monkey	prey
storey	trolley	turkey	valley

⭐ -ie-

achieve	auntie	believe	brief
calorie	cashier	diesel	drier
field	flier	frontier	grievance

hygiene	magpie	niece	piece
relief	shield	untie	zombie

⭐ -oa-

aboard	approach	boast	boat
broad	charcoal	coarse	coast
cockroach	float	goat	groan
hoard	loaf	loan	moat
poach	roast	soar	throat

⭐ -oe-

buffaloes	cargoes	doe	dominoes
foe	goes	heroes	hoe
mangoes	mistletoe	mosquitoes	mottoes
oboe	potatoes	roe	toe
tomatoes	poem	volcanoes	woe

⭐ -oi-

appoint	avoid	boil	choice
coil	coin	devoid	exploit
foil	hoist	joint	moist
noise	point	poison	oil
ointment	spoil	toilet	voice

⭐ -oo-

afternoon	balloon	bloom	boot
cartoon	cook	food	foot
gloom	good	goose	look

| loose | mushroom | noodles | poor |
| school | smooth | spool | wood |

⭐ -ou-

about	amount	announce	around
bouquet	cougar	council	count
devout	doubt	found	ghoul
group	outside	route	routine
south	souvenir	thousand	wound

⭐ -oy-

alloy	annoy	boy	buoy
convoy	corduroy	coy	decoy
deploy	destroy	employ	enjoy
envoy	foyer	joy	loyal
ploy	soya	toy	voyage

⭐ -ue

argue	avenue	barbecue	blue
continue	due	fondue	issue
overdue	pursue	rescue	residue
revue	statue	Sue	subdue
tissue	undue	value	venue

⭐ -ui-

| bruise | build | built | cruise |
| fruit | guild | guilt | guilty |

guillotine　　　guinea　　　juice　　　recruit

suit　　　suitable

⭐ **-uy-**

buy　　　guy

On your own: Ways to improve your spelling skills

To improve your spelling skills, you need to practise writing new words, see accurate models (reading is a great way to do this) and evaluate your own progress. Hopefully, the ideas below will help you accomplish this.

Create your own dictionary to help you with words you find difficult to spell or with new words you want to learn. Compile a list of ten to fifteen words. If you want, you can include diagrams and definitions for your entries. Try using the words from your dictionary in your everyday writing for class assignments and journals. Once you can spell a word from your dictionary correctly, cross the word out.

Keep track of any words you misspell in your spelling tests by writing them down on a piece of paper. Every two or three weeks, write these words on flash cards. Exchange your flash cards with a partner. Now you can quiz each other. Keep track of your progress by marking how many words you get right. If you get a word right, congratulations! If you get a word wrong, keep the flash card. Next time you may get it right!

FORTY

Index

A

B

C

I, J

K

L

M

N

O